HOW TO BE A SUCCESSFUL

Insurance Agent

GATHONI NJENGA

"Keep going. Be all in"

- Bryan Hutchinson

Copyright © 2019 by Gathoni Njenga

All rights reserved. No part of this book may be reproduced or transmitted in any form or by any means, electronic or mechanical, including photocopying, recording or by any information storage and retrieval system, without permission in writing from the publisher.

Published by Ostrich Publishers, Charlotte, North Carolina.
A Subsidiary of Corvus Web Services.
www.corvus.website

Printed In the United States of America

DESIGNED BY FRANK DAPPAH

HOW TO BE A SUCCESSFUL INSURANCE AGENT

ISBN: 9781096040668

Dedicated to all the independent Insurance Agents out there trying to build successful businesses

"It is not the critic who counts; not the man who points out how the strong man stumbles, or where the doer of deeds could have done them better. The credit belongs to the man who is actually in the arena, whose face is marred by dust and sweat and blood; who strives valiantly; who errs, who comes short again and again, because there is no effort without error and shortcoming; but who does actually strive to do the deeds; who knows great enthusiasms, the great devotions; who spends himself in a worthy cause; who at the best knows in the end the triumph of high achievement, and who at the worst, if he fails, at least fails while daring greatly, so that his place shall never be with those cold and timid souls who neither know victory nor defeat."

Theodore Roosevelt- The man in the Arena-

This book is dedicated to

Frank

Witnessing and experiencing life together

Is the

Highest honor

Of my Life.

Thank you for taking

A chance on me.

TABLE OF CONTENTS

ACKNOWLEDGMENTS			09
AUTHOR'S STORY			11
PART ONE	I	THE SALES PROCESS	15
PART TWO	I	YOUR INSURANCE SET UP	60
PART THREE	I	CREATE AN ENVIRONMENT FOR SUCCESS	73
A FINAL NOTE			106
RESOURCES			107

ACKNOWLEDGMENTS

To Bill Perry and Mo Daniels, you introduced me to whole new career. Thank you for the opportunity and thank you for being my teachers.

To Chuck Sawicki, thank you for convincing me that I wasn't crazy in my new career. Your wisdom and experience were very helpful and encouraging.

To the team at Transamerica office that we have partnered with, thank you for your support.

To Manny Degene, thank you for the support of our agency and the determination to forge a working relationship with us.

To Debbie Watkins, without you our business would not be the same. The work you do is important, and you do it superbly. Thank you.

And finally, thank you to my mom and brother, Nancy and John Njenga, who encouraged me to keep going, especially when things seemed impossible.

AUTHOR'S STORY

I started in the world of insurance by working as a direct sales associate for a major Property and Casualty Insurance company. I love the world of insurance. Academically, it's a big, interesting topic to lose yourself in and learn; if you like that sort of thing (I do!). But more importantly, few people get to see the machine or organism of the insurance company, how everything works, and the pieces fit together. I got the chance to look behind the curtain and see the invisible world that creates the insurance policies that customers purchase the world over, and it was awesome... for a while.

While the job was great, 3 years into it I began to feel really restless, and I started to question my path in this industry that I found myself in. I wanted something of my own, although, I did not know exactly what it was yet. I had a sense that there was more to life, another way to live and to create true wealth as well as a legacy. I was single, had no children and just truly felt that employment wasn't going to get me what I wanted out of life; but I was going to take the time to figure it out.

So, following this feeling, I did a very dumb thing and quit my job in 2009, with no plan or prospects, right smack in the middle of the recession. That decision greatly altered the direction of my life.

During this time, I faced many difficulties trying to figure out what I really wanted until I finally, met someone who had created what I had desired all along. That someone, was a gentleman who run a small independent Insurance agency built from the ground up, acquiring customer by customer through grit and determination. He saw something in my aspirations and decided to take a chance on me; so, I went into business with him. By this time

I had exhausted all my funds to the point where all I had was sweat, equity. and a desire to learn and work hard. The gentleman eventually became my husband, and I owe everything to him. It is such a privilege to build a business with someone you love. When we started working together, we were trying to unravel the mysteries of running an agency and how it worked overall." It was a challenging journey, to say the least, fraught with setbacks and trials, but gradually we found processes that produced consistent results. Our goal has always been to find customers and write life insurance applications weekly and finally, we came up with a process that met that goal perfectly.

In short, the reason I wrote this book, is to help other people out there with a similar dream to ours. It took us almost 5 years to figure out, a sales process that worked every time. Had there been a book in the market that explained how to get your business up and running while consistently adding to your bottom-line, reading it, and implementing the solutions, it would have taken us a much shorter time. I once heard someone call time, "**a valuable, nonrenewable resource.**" This books purpose is to save you time. It lays out what to do, when to do it, why you do it, and how to do it. It is a step by step manual to running your insurance business, which if followed, will energize your business processes and help you increase revenue.

To every agent that picks up this book, you have made a great decision, to protect clients, and families while providing for, and protecting your own. If you keep at, do the activities required, this decision will bless your life. I wish you all the best success on your journey.

PART ONE

The Sales Process

"Become the person who would attract the results you seek." - Jim Cathcart

Ground zero: Develop your Customer Profile

If you want to build a successful business, you need to have a basic idea who your; ideal customer is, and then develop a way to capture that market. The most ideal customer profile is a very narrow niche (a particular segment), and you will need to have a deep understanding of the issues that segment faces in order to serve it effectively.

For example, if you are interested in selling Medicare Supplement Plans, your ideal customer will be turning 65 or over 65, with a household income of 30k and above. Your ideal customer is retired or just about to retire, and most likely will be transitioning from a work health plan to the government Medicare system. Typically, this segment of the population is dealing with a few health problems and often go to the doctor. This means they are concerned with the rising cost of healthcare from deductibles, copays and prescriptions. If you know the issues this segment faces, then you can offer them a product that can help mitigate that cost via a Medicare supplement plan.

As another example, let's say you are interested in selling life insurance. Who will be your ideal customer? Will it be newlyweds just starting their lives out together, or perhaps business owners who need insurance on themselves, and key employees? What about older retirees who just want some insurance for final expenses? To give you an idea of what i look for in a customer, my ideal customer is at least 45 years or older, is married or single. They have children and grandchildren and live in a rural area. Once you identify the target group, the next step is to find a huge database of people in this demographic.

Step 1. Prospecting

So now that you know your ideal customer, it is time to go find them. But the question is, how?

To start, there are generally 3 kinds of prospects:

- Warm prospects- These are people you know personally.
- Referral- These are folks who have been recommended by people you know or people who have done business with you.
- Cold prospects- People you do not know.

A great prospecting plan will include prospects from each of those 3 buckets (warm, referral and cold). I would recommend, when starting out, create 2 buckets of warm and cold. Create your warm list through using your personal contacts by developing a list of 100 names who could possibly do business with you. Next, create a cold list of potential prospects who fit your customer profile. The source of a cold list would be from, for example, a lead list you can purchase such as, Salesfully.com, Infofree.com and listshack.com which all offer a monthly subscription for unlimited leads), the library or the post office.

Once you get you get your list together, I suggest you download it in a csv format so you can filter out the contacts you want to target from those you don't need. You can filter leads out with the filter tool on most database programs. Microsoft Excel, or Google sheets are relatively easy to use. Try to filter it for the specific data points you want. For instance, going back to the Medicare supplement example mentioned earlier, I would filter the list to folks turning 65 this year and search from there. The easiest way to accomplish this is would be to isolate people born in a specific year. Next, I would filter the list for; income to those making 30k and above and finally after that is complete, I would filter for the geographic area that I want to work in. Once you have your filters set, it is easy to move on to the next step.

Step 2. Decide mode of call

The goal for our agency is to make 2 to 3 appointments a day. We pick a geographical area and run appointments one day of the week and use the other 4 to prospect. To make 2 appointments from cold calls requires making 200 calls because conversion is 1%. So, for every 100 calls, you get 1 appointment. To get through 200 calls on a regular phone is pretty difficult, however, it becomes substantially easier when you load calls into a dialer that dials the numbers automatically (sometimes 2 or 3) at a time and you just answer the ones that pick up. There are plenty of companies that offer this service. At our agency we have used Callhub with great success. I would explore getting an affordable dialer for you calls.

Step 3. Getting the appointment

After I have my List of potential customers ready, and the mode of call is decided, the next step is to set up appointments with your potential customers. This may be intimidating, and you could be wondering, what to you say to them in order to get them to sit down with you. This is where scripting comes in. The most effective way I have noticed is to be direct and honest; the prospects will either say yay or nay to your proposition.

So, what is the most effective script? If you are calling cold; It should contain your name and what company you represent, the reason you are calling, and finally, it should contain a question on if they have that product in place.

Here is an example based on Medicare supplement.

"Hello, may I speak to Mrs. Jones?"

"Hi Mrs. Jones, my name is Betty from *xyz* company. The reason I am calling Mrs. Jones, is because, I am working with folks in the area who are going on Medicare this year and I wanted to see if I could help. Have you signed up for Medicare yet?"

At this point, client will either say "yes" or "no."
The next step will be a bit of education and request of the appointment.

"Great! You see, Medicare is the health plan for folks over 65 and it covers your hospital bills as well as any doctor visits, however, Medicare does not cover everything. In fact, Medicare deductibles this year are over $1300, there are supplement plans that can help you lower the cost of your health care."

"I am working in the area Friday and I can help you review your options. Will you be available?"

Client will say "yes" or "no".

For yes- "Great, do you prefer morning or afternoon? Ok I will stop by on Friday at 2 and reach out with a call to remind you on Thursday.

Thank them and hang up.

For No- "Oh what is a better time for you, Mrs. Jones.?" (**You are trying to establish if it's a time conflict, or they are not comfortable meeting with you, or it just a bad time.**)

If it's a **time conflict** suggest another time or ask them what a better time would be.

If they are **not comfortable with you yet**, ask them, "Do you have someone you trust who helps you with some of these decisions like a spouse or kids?"

Finally, ask them if they would be more comfortable if that person was present for the appointment, and book the best time to meet with them both.

If they are not interested, they will usually tell you right away. Some agents like to ask why and try to solve the issue all while hopefully booking the appointment. I prefer to move on to the next lead in order to save time. With more experience you will discover what works for you.

Script for a life insurance appointment

When it comes to setting up a life insurance appointment, everything has pretty similar scripting to the Medicare insurance.

So how does the script for life insurance go exactly?

It's very simple and direct. Just remember to be friendly and do not rush through it. Pause after each line to give the prospect time to comprehend what you are saying.

"Hello, may I speak to <Mr./Mrs. Prospect>"

"Hello, Sir/Ma'am"

"My name is <your name> with <Your Insurance company> and the reason I called today, is to inform you that, I will be working with your neighbors this week on < Their street>, and helping them with their life Insurance needs."

"I wanted the opportunity to help your family as well on your life Insurance"

"Do you currently have life insurance?"

They will answer yes or no or not interested.

If the answer is "yes", then ask a couple more questions-

"That's great that you have some coverage-Are you satisfied with the amount that you have, or would you like to look at a little more?" **Again, you get either a hesitation or "yes" or "no".** If you get a hesitation or a "yes"- a hesitations means they would like someone to look at their insurance, and they may want more but are hesitant on price, medical issues etc. What you can do here is, set up the appointment and try to solve the issue at the appointment.

Set up the appointment by saying:

"We have offer a lot of options that are affordable which I can sit down and show you when I am in the area on Friday. What time works for you morning or afternoon?"

If they are interested, they will pick one, or if they have a conflict try for another time.

You then repeat the date and time of the appointment and tell the customer that you will call them the day before to remind them of the appointment. Then thank them and hang up.

Be sure to put their information on your calendar at the time you agreed, this will ensure you never forget an appointment. I use Google calendar because I can sync it with my phone, this way even when I am on the road driving, I still have access to their name, address, and phone number readily available should I need it.

You can also ask another question that may create an opportunity for a sale-

"Are all you family members covered or ae their family members that need insurance like kids and grandkids?" There could be someone the prospect had been thinking about getting insurance for other than themselves. You can use the opportunity to set up an appointment with you in order to get that accomplished.

If you get a "no"- Just say thank you and move on. Keep working till you hit your goal for the day.

If the answer is no-to the question "do you have life insurance?" Then say," Oh? Have you ever had life insurance before?" Typically, they'll say they had it but lost it, or had it through work and retired, and no longer have it. Your objective at this time is to help the customer get their insurance back, as it is a security issue for them so try to convey that as clearly as possible by saying;

"How old are you now <Mr. and/or Mrs. Prospect>"?

Whatever they say, make light of it and respond with, "Oh so you are still pretty young!"

This simple statement always relaxes the prospective client t and eases you into asking the next question. It may seem a little intrusive but, it will provide you with a lot of information.

"Are you taking any medications at the moment?"

Why do you need to ask this question? This reminds the customer that insurance is not a product you can just go out and get. All potential clients will need a professional guide to help them find the right one. You are the consultant- and it shifts the dynamic where the potential clients start to see you as a professional.

So, by this time if the client is taking medication, probably they are aware that insurance is not that straightforward when it comes to some health conditions. They are almost always discouraged at this point. Your job now is to offer hope that you can help them; because you know that you can! To proceed, say the previous line you have used before;

"< Mr. and Mrs. prospect> I will be happy to help you get back some insurance. We have a lot of options available that would work for you and I can sit down and show you when I am in the area on Friday. What is a good time to stop by, morning or afternoon?"

Usually they will pick a good time, at which point, repeat the information back to them and let know you will call them the day before to remind them of the appointment. Thank them, hang up and move onto the next call after recording their information on your calendar. Finally, you are ready to move on to the final step before proceeding with the actual appointment.

Step 4- Confirm the appointment

The day before the appointment occurs, call to confirm with client that everything is set for the meeting. Again, you will need a script here as the prospective client may not be sold yet on the appointment.

A script needs to be short and to the point, containing only the pertinent information but familiar enough to make the client comfortable.

Here is an example;

"Hey, may I speak to Mrs. Jones? Mrs. Jones, this is Betty from *xyz*. I just wanted to remind you of our Medicare/Life Insurance appointment tomorrow at 10, do you still live at (insert address)? Great, looking forward to meeting with you tomorrow at 10, take care."

Note. If the customer says yes to the question of the address, they have also said another yes to the appointment, so you are ready to move on to the next step.

Step 5: The appointment

For most sales people, this is the favored part of the whole process. The overall tone of the appointment should be positive and friendly in a "getting to know each other "kind of way. There are a few key elements to getting yourself prepared. For Instance, look professional, carry some identification in case a customer needs to see it and make sure you have your applications ready or your quoting/application software updated.

The overall goal of an appointment is to get a sale or a commitment to a sale and get referrals. So how do you accomplish these objectives? First and foremost. the way you get a sale or referral is by asking pertinent questions that will uncover opportunities on how you can help. Follow the outlining steps below to have a success appointment flow.

There are four parts to an appointment

- Establish Rapport

- Provide Information and Value proposition

- Close the sale or get the commitment to close the sale

- Getting the referral

Establish Rapport

In most appointments, the first thing you want to do is make the prospect comfortable and establish rapport. Usually the easiest and most genuine way to establish rapport is to allow the prospect to talk about their family, kids, and grandkids. Ask about their hobbies, what they enjoy doing in their spare time, and share your hobbies as well in order to form some common ground. Give genuine compliments to the prospect, notice any pictures and sports trophies lying around, and ask about them; let the prospect brag on their own and their family's accomplishments.
Rapport building allows you to ask deeper, more personal questions about a customer's financial or health situations, their worries, and concerns and additionally, this is the information you will use later on to recommend a product tailored specifically for them.

Some sample questions

"Did you grow up in this town?"

"What made you move here?"

"Do your children live in the same town.?"

"Do you get to see them often?"

"How did you end up working in this industry?"

"What do like best about it?"

"You must be really happy to retire, what do you do in your spare time?"

"I see you have some golfing pictures- how long have you been golfing?"

"What do you like about it."

"What has been your best score."

Transition to more serious questions

"The reason I stopped by is because you said you were interested in (Insert Insurance Product), do you have any coverage at the moment?"

If the answer is no. "What is the reason you wanted to take care of this now?"

If the answer is yes. "What is the reason you are still looking for coverage?"

"Are you currently taking medications?"

"What are you taking the medications for?"

"When were you diagnosed with that condition?"

"Which doctor do you see for these conditions?"

"How often do you see them?"

As you can see the whole point of rapport building is to get the prospect comfortable to answer the more pertinent questions about existing coverage. Once you have gathered enough information, it will be easier to proceed with useful guidance and information.

Provide Information and Value Proposition

The purpose of providing information is to show the client what coverage is appropriate for them using your existing product knowledge. You would begin by telling the client that based on what information they have provided about their current health and financial circumstances they have a few choices of coverage. Be careful not to overwhelm the customer with too many options. Keep the number of choices high enough to provide options yet narrow enough to focus the customer on making a selection. It is for that reason that, I prefer to give the customer **three** different choices. Explain what each choice of coverage is offering, both advantages as well as disadvantages, and finally make your recommendation out of those three choices provide giving the reason why based on the questions you had asked previously.

For example:

"With your current situation, Betty, I recommend (choice 3) because, even though you are taking (medication) you are still able to medically qualify and get accepted for this coverage. The coverage would start on day 1 with no waiting period, covering you immediately- so you don't have to burden your family financially if anything happened to you. Also, Betty, since you are on a fixed income, you will be glad to know the price of the insurance will stay the same and never go up on you, and the coverage will stay the same and never diminish."

If the customer has any questions here, fully address the question before you move on to the next phase. This section is a very important step, as it is where the prospect agrees with you that the coverage you have selected for them is best for them; and therefore, decide on whether or not they will buy from you. To do that, the client will have to fully understand the product and how it applies to **them** as an individual. I would recommend that you take your time and check back with the client, to make sure they are fully engaged, interested, and understand the coverage.

Once clarification has been accomplished, I would explain how the process works, tell the client, what to expect and confirm how to pay for the coverage. If you get any resistance here, it is important to address each issue before you move onto the next step.

Here is an example on how to proceed:
"So, to set up this coverage, Betty, I need to go through an application with you. The application will ask you a few medical questions about your medication and any treatments that you are currently on. You also need to decide on the date you would like to pay your bill. The insurance gives you an option to choose the date based on when that they draft your account anywhere between the 1st to the 28th, so choose the date that is the most convenient for you. Next, the company will pull your medical records from your doctor and compare the answers listed on the application to what's on your medical records; then they will either approve or deny coverage. When they approve coverage, they will bill your bank account for the

premium. If the deny coverage they will send you a letter informing you of that decision. This whole entire process takes about 4 weeks so if you get approved, your first payment will be next month. Does that sound ok to you"?

Close the sale or get commitment for the sale

Once you are sure the prospect fully understands the product and that they want it, you will now be able to calculate the amount they want and how much they can actually afford. Most insurance agents make the mistake of trying to sell the biggest coverage to prospects, however, that's a really short-term view. You want the prospect to be able to pay for a policy long term so that it can benefit them and eventually, benefit you. You do not want the client to get coverage that is a struggle for them to pay every as month that will eventually lapse, leaving your prospect uninsured and you with a chargeback from the insurance company.

So, the best strategy here is to make a recommendation of what coverage that they need, the reason why, and if they are comfortable with the price; then **undersell**. The undersell does 3 things; First, it makes the client know you are looking out for them, you just want them to be protected, but only at a price they can manage comfortably. Secondly, it gives them a way to admit something may be too expensive for them without embarrassment. And third, if they can manage the price, it makes them recommit to the product at that price (usually you will hear a statement like, " Oh I can manage that," or " I believe that will be fine," or sometimes they may ask for more coverage because they have realized they can comfortably afford it.

The selling statement would go like:

"Betty, ultimately you want to get coverage that you can keep and manage with the rest of your bills comfortably. For final expenses in this area, a funeral and final bills range between 12-15k. For your age and health, a 15k policy would run you ($) a month. How does that feel for you? (**Pause and listen to what they say here, look at body language for signs of comfort or discomfort**).

Next, reinforce the first statement.

"Is that a price you can comfortably pay every month, or would you prefer for me to look for something smaller that you can manage? Having some coverage is better than not having any at all, so we will go with whatever you are comfortable with."

(Listen for the buying signal here, which is usually, I think I can manage that). Next, confirm what the customer wants by this statement.

"Are you ok with the 15k or would you like me to look at higher or lower coverage."

After this statement the customer will choose their option then you quickly set it up. The phrasing around this would go something like:

"Ok Betty you have decided on the 15k at ($) so, I will fill out the application. I will be asking legal and medical questions, and just stop me if you are unclear about anything."

Just begin filling out the application, keeping it simple and straightforward, and get all the information that is required on the application. Once the app is complete, go through the application page by page and get all the signatures so that: **1.** The customer sees that it is a real application , **2.** The customer visually sees, the information asked is part of the application, **3.** reinforce the process you had described earlier.

Referrals

Referrals is one of those things you absolutely must do in your business to stay in business. Your sale will feed you today, but referrals will feed you in the future. Also, one customer only equals one sale while referrals give you a multiple on that sale. There is no magic number of referrals you should get; however, you should aim for a minimum of 3 to replace the sale you just made. In my experience, one in three will work out since people do not usually know their friends' and neighbors' financial conditions. By giving you the referral, they are only guessing that you may help them. So, when should you ask for referrals? What do you say? At what point of the sale do you bring this referral conversation up?

Let's tackle when to ask for referrals first. The answer simply is, when you prove yourself worthy. Understand that the clients, love their friends and family, and if they recommend someone it has to be someone who they think is knowledgeable and can be trusted. In my opinion, after the customer has committed to the policy and given you everything necessary to get the policy activated, then they have proven they trust you; considering they have given you their personal information, their health, their banking, etc. And so, because they trust you, **tell** them you can provide the same service to their friends and family. You should never, ever feel guilty about asking for a referral as you are providing a service that the customer needs. If you can help them, then you can help their loved ones in a similar situation. So, to summarize, the referral is not about you, it's about them providing value to your client's loved ones.

An example of a referral statement would go like this:
"Betty, I am going to take care of your policy for you to make sure that you and your family are protected. I hope I have answered all of your questions and that you trust me enough to provide the same protection for your family- who do you know that has no coverage or need coverage?"

Follow Ups

The follow up process is the easiest step in the sales process to mess up. The reason I say this is because it requires pure discipline to follow ups and it is systematic; not to mention most people find it mind- numbingly boring. Despite this fact, it is vital to follow up because some customers just do not do business on the first call. It may be a bad time for them, or they may not be sure about the product, or you so following up allows you to win their trust and answer any questions that may come up. To the sales person following up, this process provided an opportunity to sell more and therefore, make more money.

So how do you follow up with a customer?

Usually, the customer will tell you right away if it's a bad time to do business because of a certain reason. Once you determine that the reason is genuine, then offer your empathy and suggest a time frame that would be more appropriate.

For example:

Betty says, "I do not have the coverage I need right now but I have some bills I am working on paying, then I can get some coverage."

Advisor answers, "I hear you Betty, sometimes you have to take care of bills to get you in a secure position that will allow you to keep your coverage once you get it. Would it be ok to call and check on you in 2 months or so?"

Betty answers, "Yes I want the coverage, but I can't afford to take it out now, yes please check on me in 2 months"

Advisor responds, "Ok Betty, I will hold you to it! I will check on you in 2 months so we can get you the protection you need, till then take care."

The next step is to note it in your calendar with everything you can remember about the call, so when you speak to Betty in two months, you will remember some details about her and what she needed. The details aid in 2 things, 1. Re-establishing the rapport you had previously built and 2.

Convey to the customer that you care, and you keep your word and therefore, are trustworthy.

In two months call your prospect saying:

"Hi Betty, this is (your name), I called because we had spoken 2 months ago about your insurance. We have added some new type of policies that might work for you and your family; I would love to show them to you. I was working in your area on (insert date). Will you be available that day?"

The client will either 1. set up the appointment 2. reschedule or 3. tell you they are not interested.

1. **If they set up the appointment-** then you got what you originally wanted, which is a chance to resell.
2. **If they reschedule-** set up another follow up call.
3. **If they say they are not interested-** say "I certainly understand, Betty. I wanted to see how I can help. Now, let's' think of anybody who could benefit from insurance, I would love to be able to help them. Who do you know that needs coverage?"

To answer the question of how many times you should follow up, in my experience, if the customer is showing some interest, follow up till they buy or until they tell you they are not interested.

Step 6. Submitting the application and the Importance of a good agency coordinator or AA

Congratulations! You have successfully contacted a prospect, they made the appointment, you made the sale, and filled out an application. The next part of the process is to submit the policy to the insurance company and hopefully get it approved. This will allow the customer to get covered, you are compensated, and everybody is happy. The process will only be straight forward if you submit a perfect application, with absolutely no mistakes. Otherwise, the mistakes will have to be corrected before an application can be approved; which then means going back to the customer's house to fix the issue. Mistakes could mean, a number of things such as, forgetting a signature or answering a question incorrectly. It's always awkward to go back to the customer to correct an error, not to mention, it is perilous to your sale; and every time you must do it, the closer you get to loosing that sale. Look at the situation from the customer's view to get a better idea of the scenario. When they fill out the application, in their mind the process is done and consider themselves to have completed something that had been nagging at them for a long time. Every time you come to them, with a mistake to fix, they are reminded that the process is not done, everything seems more complicated, and they begin to doubt your competence. Many customers have at this point said, "you know what, forget about it!"

So how do you prevent this kind of mess? I would urge you to fill out every question on the application. Before you leave the client's home, review the application to make sure you did not miss anything. When you get to the office, review it again then hand that application to the agency coordinator or an administrative assistant to double-check everything.

A good agency coordinator, or AA, is worth their weight in gold!! That is not an exaggeration. What they do is scrub your application and catch anything that is out of order with the policy before it is submitted to underwriting. Usually the AA will follow up with underwriting to push an application through to approval. They will coordinate with the agent to make sure that the underwriter's questions and outstanding requirements are fulfilled. It is very easy to see how, without them, many policies would not be issued, agents and insurance companies would not be as successful, and far less people would have insurance. The AA's are the ones that make insurance companies run together like a well- oiled machine. They are of tremendous value to agents, agency managers, and underwriters alike.

In short, develop a working relationship with the coordinators of the agency or the insurance company. They are all very well trained, but the ones with the most experience are usually the best, having seen all sorts of applications and policies. Most likely have memorized the underwriting guidelines of what is permissible and what is not, making your job a lot easier. Running some customer scenarios by them might, such as, a case that seems hopeless, might be beneficial to you, they usually have a suggestion on how to get that person covered. All in all, a good agency coordinator will add tremendous value to your business.

Step 7: Delivery

After the policy has been submitted to underwriting, that department will, go through the process of verifying the customer's medical and personal history. If everything checks out, they will approve the policy and send it you, your office, or the customer directly. The best process is to always deliver the insurance policies yourself. There are 2 reasons for that. Firstly, delivering the policy yourself, completes the sales loop for you and the customer. For the customer, they got a call from a stranger, sat down with them, gave them their information and 4 weeks later the stranger (agent) delivers the policy and they are insured. By delivering the policy you are walking the customer through the process of successfully applying for insurance and completing the job. Secondly, doing this step yourself improved the stickability factor of the policy. A policy sent in the mail is just a piece of mail, with nothing memorable about it. When you deliver a policy, go over the coverage, and reassure the client that they are taken care of, you are in essence reselling the policy and confirming to them that they made the right decision. This Increases the chances of them keeping that policy in place exponentially.

Delivering the policy is also another opportunity to ask for more business. You have proved to be a man/woman of your word and trustworthy, which means the family members and friends will get the same courteous treatment and service. So, say, "Betty, I am so glad that you trusted me to help you with your insurance coverage. Your family is now more protected because of the decisions that you made. I would love to help your family members in the same way that I helped you. Do you have family members that you think might need some help with insurance?" If they are not able to think about any one right away, prompt them by saying, "are all the grandkids insured? We have some really great children policies that parents, or grandparents, can take out to protect the little ones and start building a legacy for the family."

The referral process may or may not get you some leads, but you should always say your referral statement; and here is why. When worked correctly, referral business adds 16% in sales to the bottom line. So, if you consistently bring up referrals, you will get 16% more business than if you never brought up referrals. Don't leave money on the table, make it part of your process, and always bring up referrals with every customer at every delivery.

Once you deliver the policy and get referrals, let the client know that you will continue to service the policy. You will need to set up an annual review of their insurance needs so, at that time get your calendar and schedule the annual review a year from that date. Be sure to inform the client that you will call to remind them closer to that date. The reason for scheduling the review is, simply that, if you do not make it an automatic practice, it's pretty easy to forget to set up the annual review, especially as your client list starts to grow and you get more, and more busy. By scheduling a year in advance, you will;

1. Have an opportunity to touch base with the customer and solidify in your mind that you are their agent.
2. Have the opportunity to sell more coverage to their family.

Make These Procedures Work for You.

1. Have a prospecting plan with the three kinds of prospects; warm (friends and family), cold (from lead lists) and referrals (from prior business)

2. Use a dialer to get through a lot of calls at one time.

3. Have a script ready to go once the prospect answers the phone.

4. Confirm all appointments the day before the appointment.

5. Master the appointment flow.

6. To issue your policies faster, be careful to make not make mistakes on your

applications, and closely work with your AA and Agency coordinator.

7. Deliver your policy in person and be sure to ask for referrals.

PART TWO

YOUR INSURANCE SET UP

"If you don't know where you are going, you will end up somewhere else." Yogi Berra

Your Book of Business

A book of business put simply, is a collection of clients and their accounts. It is your client collection and contains a list of all the insurance policies that you have written. Each client or policy generates a commission and therefore has an assigned value.

It is very important to keep track of your customers and their policies so that:

1. You can Identify which areas/ families are generating best sales.

2. Identify opportunities of cross-selling and upselling.

3. Identify who to call to get more referrals and therefore increase sales.

4. Help you determine who and where to market in the future to drive growth of your business.

Future Value of Your Book

Since a book of business is a list of clients and the revenue they generate in the form of commissions, the book has value that can be traded. For example, let's say your modest book of business generates gross commissions of 60k a year. This may cause, other insurance agents to be interested in purchasing your book of business for various reasons. A few examples of why a financial professional may want to purchase your book may be;

1. A desire to expand their existing business and revenue.
2. They are new agents in the business who would prefer to start with an income right away while they build up their business instead of starting from scratch.

On average insurance books are available on the market for 2*annual gross commissions. So, working from the example previously, a book that generates 60k annually would sell for (on average) 2*$60, 000= $120,000.

Some advice- Building a book of business requires patience and diligence on selling insurance policies every single week. If you are consistent, you will see the value of your book grow. If you are not following the steps- {prospect, appointments, sales, follow up} and being consistent week after week, you will find yourself starting over every time and eventually burn out. In short, keep your business simple and just go get it. Follow the process and combine it with the right volume of appointments to successfully close business every single week; trust the system and the law of numbers.

Getting Appointed with The Right Insurance Company

When you are starting your insurance career, it's very important to think about your business partner (the insurance co) and what kind of relationship you want with them. There are 2 types of Independent agent appointments.

Direct Appointments

Indirect

They both have advantages and disadvantages, which I will discuss.

Direct Appointments

A direct appointment is a legal agreement where the agent receives authorization to act for the insurance company as an agent without any secondary parties. The agent's responsibility is to sell and service policies on behalf of the company, and for that the agent receives commission directly from the insurance company. The advantage of this relationship is you will have access to the insurance products that can build your customer base and your book of business independently. You can be contracted with more than one company at the same time, all while deciding which product works best for your client among the offerings that you have. You get to claim ownership of your book of business, which you can sell in the future. Additionally, any commissions or residuals do not have to be shared with a third party, meaning you do all the work and get paid all your money. The disadvantages are;

1. The biggest complaint from independent agents is there is no support, sales assistance or training is limited. For a new agent trying to out the industry, the whole processes can be quite challenging in the beginning, causing most agents to give up. I would suggest having a brain trust of a group of people who have been **successful** in the industry to call on for when times get difficult or when you need some advice. I stress successful, because successful people are usually positive, encouraging, and know that what you are

trying to achieve is possible because they have done it themselves. Stay away from taking advice from those that have not been able to make things work, their advice will reflect this negative mindset. Don't allow them to steal your dream before it's realized. Another tip is read, read and read some more, inhale information about the industry, what people are doing and subscribe to insurance magazines- you may find a solution to the issue you are having in your business.

2. It is also quite difficult to get a direct appointment if you do not have much experience. I would suggest getting a list of all insurance companies appointed in your state and call them to ask for a direct appointment. Usually, they will tell you if they do or don't; just toss side those that don't. Even If, the top-rated carriers may not want to take a gamble on you right now., don't let it discourage you. The idea is to get appointed and start

selling. You can revisit the big brands later when you

have experience and a book of business.

Indirect Appointments

Sometimes agents partner up with agencies known as, IMO's (independent marketing organization) or senior agents who get them appointed with an insurance company for a cut of your business and commission. For simplicity, we will call agencies, **IMO's** and senior agents a **group**. The advantage of these groups is that you can get a lot of support from seasoned agents that will teach you the business from beginning to end. Usually, the groups have support staff, that will take a look at your applications, submit them for you, follow up with underwriting, and make sure the insurance is issued which allows everybody to get paid (i.e. you and your partner, the group).

The disadvantages are:

1. Most of the time you will be restricted from selling for other insurance co or groups, your contract with the group will let you know.
2. You may not own your book of business, and you will have to look at your contract to confirm. You may be

building the groups book of business and if you decide to part ways, you cannot take your customers with you, or sometimes the book that you develop will be owned by you and the group so you may not be able to sell it when you decide you want to get out of the business.

3. You do not make maximum commissions because you are sharing with a third party; meaning when you start out, you may not know what commissions are fair and what are not. For example, on average a life insurance company will pay an agent 100% first year commission to the agent for a whole life policy and 4% residuals for 10 years. So, if you are signed up with a secondary party, they do an **assignment of commission** where they assign themselves a % of the proceeds. Some groups can assign themselves any percentage. I have seen 30-70% assignment to the group and the agent gets the rest. You need to decide what is fair **before** you sign your contract, so ask the group to clarify what

their **override** (industry speak for assignment of commission) is.

Some advice

I would suggest that you write up a business plan for your insurance career. Most Insurance agents start out with an indirect appointment (sometimes intentionally or unintentionally).

I have a friend who intentionally started out in a group because he wanted the training and the opportunity to learn the insurance agents processes in order to replicate it in his own agency. He was with the group for 9 months before heading off on his own, and at that time he made a point to, set up direct appointments with different insurance carriers. He has been very successful ever since all because he had a really good foundation at the start of his business.

One can also unintentionally start out in a group. Usually some people start out in insurance because someone sold them an opportunity or recruited them. When someone brings you into their business, they will teach you how be a successful agent and for that, expect to be compensated by the override. So long as everything is out in the open, and there is consent, it can be a mutually rewarding experience. However, there are some bad apples in the industry that tend to not disclose the assignment of commission or the ownership of the book of business. You do not want to start working with someone only to get surprised on the actual commission split between you and them later on. In addition, this may cause you not own the customers you have sold to and therefore be unable to take your customers with you when you decide to leave. In order to not waste your time and your efforts, it is critical to understand that it is **your responsibility to read** and **understand** insurance contracts and agreements between you and any third party. If the information in the contract is not clear, speak to someone who can explain it you in order to avoid inadvertently making a mistake.

"Leave no stone unturned"

-Euripides

PART THREE

CREATE AN ENVIRONMENT FOR SUCCESS

"Every skill you acquire doubles your odds for success." Scott Adams

Skill one: How to set up your day

Everyone knows that in order to be successful in your project or career, you must have a clear vision of what you want and then go after it. So, in this insurance industry, what is the optimum schedule that, if followed, will lead to some measure of success? The answer is to keep things very simple, **only worry about 2 things**, prospecting and making appointments.

When you read insurance magazines, blogs and books, state that you need to **know your why.** Why do you do what you do? The answers vary from helping families, creating something greater than yourself, or to serving the community, etc. All those things *are nice*, but they are not practical tools that will get you what you want. What you need to remember your job activity is mostly prospecting. You are in the prospecting business not the Insurance business. According to

Nick Murray who wrote "The game of numbers-Professional Prospecting for Financial Advisers "(pg. 104) he states that:

"If you are starting out, you will need to be prospecting no less than:

80% of your time in years one and two

70% of your time in year three

60% of your time in year four

50% in year five"

If you follow this formula, you will be successful in the business. Please note you need at least 5 years in the business **consistently, working every day** to see the big financial benefit. **"There is no substitute for hard work"- Thomas Edison**
To make best use of your time, to incorporate the prospecting activities needed to achieve your objectives, I would recommend you use this daily schedule as a guideline.

A sample work schedule

8:00-9:00   Read an Insurance magazine, or financial services book

9:00-11:00   Make your Cold Calls-Act natural on the phone

11:00- 11:30   Break

11:30-1:30   Make your warm calls/ if you don't have any cold call

1:30- 2:30   Lunch

2;30-4.30   Do all your follow ups, call backs etc.

5:00- 6.00   Go for networking events- introduce yourself and collect business cards-these will be prospected to later.

The goal of this workflow is to make 2 appointments a day. I would suggest you make the appointments for 1 day of the week, which you would then designate as your appointment day. This will allow for 4 days prospecting for appointments uninterrupted.

Skill two: The Sunday Night Set Up

"By failing to prepare, you are preparing to fail,"- Benjamin Franklin

Sunday night is a great time to plan out your week. You should try and collect all you need for the week and have the details ready to go by Monday morning. What exactly do you need? First you should figure out the geographic area that you will be working in for that week. Next you need to download a list of prospects in that area. Typically for a successful week I like to have 4 call days and one appointment day, which is usually Friday. The goal is to have 8-10 appointments by Friday; therefore, you will need at least 1000 names to call. You would get your lead list from lead companies like Salesfully or Infofree, download them and prep them for the dialer (I use Callhub). Prepping the leads would be getting rid of unnecessary data and leaving only pertinent information. For example, the first name, last name, address, phone number and age. Once the data is scrubbed, it is loaded and saved on to the dialer. This whole process takes a couple of hours but the advantage of getting it done on Sunday night is;

1. By Monday morning you are ready to get to work there is no need to waste time scrambling looking for leads and uploading them.
2. It does something to the mind when you have all the tools ready to do a job, creating a sense of peace and focus. I would argue that you sleep better on Sunday night by reducing any, restlessness, when you prepare ahead of time.

Another part of preparation is looking at your existing client list and making notes of selling opportunities existing in the client's lives. For example, a client may ask, "If I get this amount of insurance now, can I add on more coverage later?" This statement means, that while the customer cannot afford the coverage they really want today, they may be able to do so in the future. Make a note to check back in 6 months to a year and fulfill the need for the client.

Once you look over the selling opportunities, make a list of customers you want to contact and meet with and schedule the calls on your calendar.

At the end of the day, you will have your cold list ready and your warm list scheduled on your calendar. The only thing left to do is execute on the plan. If you follow this process consistently on a weekly basis, it frees up most of your days for marketing activities, and therefore leads to more generating consistent income from these marketing activities.

Skill three: Prospecting (cold-call) Challenges and how to overcome them

Prospecting is the life blood of the insurance and financial services/sales profession. It is impossible to grow your business without it. It is also the cheapest way to market/talk to a lot of people for very little money. When starting out, prospecting is also the most challenging thing to do every day. Initially, prospecting does not feel natural, at all. All agents I have spoken to admit that in the beginning of their career, prospecting produced anxiety, and most have confessed that every time they got a no from a prospect, it really knocked their confidence.

While this may be discouraging, there is good news! Prospecting is a muscle that you must exercise, and the more you do it, the better you will become. There are some recommendations to consider that can make prospecting easier. I am a big fan of cold calling, especially if you do not have social connections, or your network just won't or (can't) buy from you.

I would recommend you cold call with a friend or colleague who is in the business with you. When I first started cold calling, I was petrified. My words came out flat or sometimes my voice was so high, I did not sound natural at all, thankfully, I had someone in the room with me who was more experienced in cold calling so they would give me tips like slowing down the script so the prospect can hear you clearly. When someone hung up on me, initially I would get so mad, (I mean how rude!!) but working in a room where everyone is experiencing the same thing, it becomes funny after a while and eventually you realize it's part of the game. That helped me learn to not take it personally. Inevitably, you will get someone who will hear you out but say no in the end. Keep in mind they are not saying no to you personally (because they do not know you), they are saying no because of their circumstances (they may not be able to afford it, or have a lot going on in their family, or may have already taken care of it). The best thing you can do is thank them and move on to the next prospect. Remember, it takes

100 calls to make 1 appointment, so if you need 2, be prepared to make 200 calls.

The next thing that will make or break your business is consistency. I would recommend not ending your day until you have at least 2 appointments on your calendar. In the beginning, every day counts, every appointment count, so you have to put in an extraordinary amount of effort to start the sales cycle and keep it going. Trust that the numbers will work out in your favor and keep pushing forward.

To keep in mind --Some agent behavior/attitudes about cold calling that are not productive. Since cold calling is perceived as brutal, some agents decide that it doesn't work and will concentrate on working their social leads only. I believe this is not the case because
concentrating on who you know as the only means of prospecting is not productive and doesn't work in the long run. We know a limited amount of people, to get 2 appointments a

day for 5 years, you need thousands of leads to generate 8-10 appointments a week. Unless you have a social network of 250,000 people a year, you need to hit the cold market to make your numbers. Work with organizations like **Infofree, Salesfully, and Listshack** who will give you bulk contacts for a relatively low monthly price to add on new names to your prospect list.

Great Habits that Clients Appreciate and Reward

Do your clients a solid, always tell the truth.

Tell you clients the truth even if they do not want to hear it, or it is uncomfortable to say. Usually in the life insurance business, people who have had health challenges may be rejected or rated up by the insurance co. It's never nice to deliver this kind of news to the customer. I have seen agents start avoiding customer calls because they have to tell them bad news. To avoid this awkwardness, get as much information about the client's health during the appointment, take a look at their medication and then tell them, "**Insurance companies will look into your medical history to make a decision on the policy. Sometimes it's better to tell the company up front anything you are concerned about so the information in your history matches. Otherwise, they may turn you down if they get information that surprises them. Or worse, approve the insurance and if you were to pass away because of a health issue they were not aware of, your family could have a hard

time with the claim." This statement makes it safe for the client to tell you everything on their health.

Once you have the full all the information, it is then safe to give your quote. If the policy will be rated up because of health issues, let the client know it's because of their health and every insurance company will rate them based on their health status. Say something like, "(first name), I am concerned about the cancer diagnosis you had a few years ago, although I am glad you are doing better. For all insurance companies, your health and medical history affects the price of your insurance and based on your health the price is (amount of dollars). Once the cancer is in remission about 5 years, then you will be eligible for a rate change because your health will be better." The point of this statement is to give the information in a matter of factually but kind manner, and clients usually remember that when recommending you to their friends.

Undersell

When it comes to Insurance most customers want a lot of it, so this becomes a very sobering conversation once they discover how much it costs; especially at a later age. If a customer is set on having a specific amount of insurance and is confronted with the price of it, they will do one of 2 things;

1. Shut down and give up on the whole insurance idea, because they can't afford it, or;

2. Take the insurance out of guilt, even though it will be a financial stress on them.

I suggest you have a very frank conversation, with those that can't afford it to explain that the price of the insurance is based on the customer's age and health. Empathize that you understand their dilemma and explain they don't have to get the large amount; they could get what they can manage a month, so that their family has some protection instead of none as **something is better than nothing**.

For those who may purchase out of guilt, explain what happens those who that take out insurance policies that are a financial stress. They always lapse within a few months, resulting in the customer being unprotected as well as losing all the premiums that they initially paid to set up the policy. Give the clients an alternative and suggest starting off with a policy that they can pay for comfortably. If they want to add on more coverage in a year, you will be back to set it up.

The advantage in this strategy is, your approach is customer focused and customized for the client and their financial situation, additionally, you get an opportunity to revisit the customer in a year and build a relationship with that family, which will help you uncover more opportunities of service.

Take an Interest in Family Members

When you are at a client appointment, look around the house. Most families display family portraits, graduation pictures, baby pictures, and kids' trophies. Ask you customers about them. Does your prospect light up when they talk about their kids and grandkids? If so, ask more questions like what their kids do, or where they live, and pretty soon you will have an accurate map of the family. Then, look for opportunities of service. For example, if you notice your prospect has some grandkids and college seems to be important to the family, say something like," **Kids' life policies are relatively cheap. They protect the child and start building the child's financial future early on. Some can even be structured so they can help pay for a child's college.** "Most clients appreciate such information and if they are able, start thinking about those options and set them up when they are ready.

Manage your finances- Put away 6-12 Months living Expenses

When most people are starting out in the insurance industry, they tend to come from an employment background where they get a paycheck every week, or every 2 weeks, so jumping into a commission only environment can be quite a culture shock where your earning is based on your own levels of activity and sales. Your income is never guaranteed, and you don't have the assurance and security of a check in the future.

This lack of a guaranteed check, or mental safety net can make every client appointment anxiety inducing because you have a lot at stake. That anxiety can make agents come off as desperate to sell, or worse, sell to customers based on your personal bills or needs and as opposed to customer's actual insurance needs.

It is very difficult to do a good job for your client if you are in a financially vulnerable position. The business is stressful and if you go long enough without sales, it very likely that you will throw in the towel. To save yourself from the stress, sacrifice a portion of your commissions and transfer it your 6-12 month living expenses fund, start with 10% and on those months, you make more, transfer more until you meet your goal. With the living expense safety net, you will notice, you can be more relaxed, and when you are relaxed, you actually sell more. Being happier and feeling more in control of your circumstances, helps substantially in a self-sustained career.

Purchase Life Insurance for Yourself

When you practice what you preach and purchase life insurance, that experience becomes a very powerful selling tool, and can help you overcome objections. One of the most common objections that you will run across is affordability. If you have a personal story relating to affordability and purchasing insurance, there is usually a shift in the client's mindset because they can relate to your story and your experience. I usually say (this is my exact experience), "**You know, when I first started in this business 7-8 years ago, it was in the middle of the recession. I was flat broke, with barely any living money, no savings, no insurance at all, no health, and no life. I was starting literally from the bottom. I was really vulnerable, but I knew that I needed some insurance, so I got what I could (10000- whole life). I will never forget it because that's all I could afford every month; so, I knew no matter how tough things got, I could keep that insurance. And what do you know, because I got insurance within my budget, I still have that policy till today. Seven years have just flown by, and it even has some cash value now. Why don't we start off with an amount that can protect you and provide the knowledge that during rough times or when things are good, your insurance will stay in place. Later, when things get better financially, we can add on a little more, does that sound reasonable?"

Most clients will be nodding their heads in agreement when you are genuine and honest, so recommend to the clients whatever you have in place for yourself and family. They will follow suit.

October-December Catch Up

After working hard, the entire year, by this time you may have some customers, that are still in your book of business or some have lapsed completely, (that's part of the business). You will most likely have a whole bunch of contacts that didn't work out. Collect all those contacts in a database and give them a courtesy call starting in October and saying, **"Hi, (prospect/client), this is (your name) with (your company). I was calling to check on you because we are getting ready to start wrapping up the year. I wanted to see if you are happy with your insurance."**

What this activity does is:

1. Help reconnect with your client and solidify your position as their agent.
2. Catch potential changes they want on their policy.
3. Enable you to add some more insurance if desired.
4. Allow the client to refer you to a family member.

Either way, when you add this step to your annual sales calendar, you will uncover opportunities for sales. Not connecting with your customers at this time, would be a missed opportunity to your bottom line and will leave your customers vulnerable to other agents who may come calling with an offer to do an "free annual review of their policies."

Single Tasking and being Present

To do something well, you have to exert a great deal of effort, focus, and consistency in order to see some kind of positive result. Unfortunately, in today's modern world (especially in the age of social media), there are a million things that are fighting for our time and attention. The result is a diminished capacity to focus, which can be disastrous when you are in a sink or swim environment like sales, entrepreneurship, or self-employment. In this world, you instantly pay for your mistakes in terms of revenue/cash. It is **unforgiving** and relentless to those with a lack of attention, focus or drive. To improve your focus, I suggest single tasking. Single tasking is the practice of dedicating oneself to a single task and minimizing potential interruptions till the task is completed. This will ensure you give 100% to your tasks and avoid missing any vital steps.

During prospecting or making your calls, make a point to always, put away your cell phone and close all browsers on your computer except your (calendar and your calling software). You will notice that when you single-task, you will make your appointments faster, and you will be able to listen to prospects more, and therefore connecting. When you are not focused, or distracted by social media for example, you tend to make mistakes on the scripting. A prospect can tell when you are distracted and not actively listening, which leads to less appointments and more time spent making appointments. If it takes longer to make an appointment, you spend more money on your calling software as most charge by the minute.

Please do not pull out your cell phone and start scrolling through various fields or take any calls (business or personal) during an appointment with a customer, even if they are your close friend or family member. It is so disrespectful to a customer to not pay attention to them, and that behavior sends a message that you do not take yourself seriously, or you are incompetent and are taking their business for granted. Discussing life insurance is a serious discussion and should be treated with the careful consideration it deserves. I have seen agents' loose sales by paying more attention to their phone rather than the client. Think about it. It costs money to make an appointment, it costs money to go to the appointment in terms of transportation, and in order to get a return on the money you have invested, the least you can do is focus on one thing only; your customer's needs. If you think you are going to be tempted to look at your phone out of force of habit, put your phone in your bag, and keep it out of view. That way you do not accidentally and subconsciously offend your client.

When taking the life application, please do only that activity and nothing else. There are a lot of questions to fill out and it's really easy to make a mistake or miss a signature. Slow all the way down and take your time to fill out the application correctly. Filling out an application incorrectly will cause delays in the policy being issued and, sometimes, you may have to go back to the customer's house to correct the application, which then causes delays in your compensation. So, getting this step right is **critical to your livelihood.** Do not get distracted by anything else, just do this one task, complete it, double/triple check the application to make sure you have all your signatures, and get all questions answered before you leave.

Appearance

There is a quote that says, 'First Impressions are the most lasting." - English proverb. It takes 10 seconds for the human mind to make a judgement on appearance. Appearance speaks volumes about you, your intelligence, professionalism. You can use this fact to your advantage. When meeting with clients you want to look your best. Doing so, makes you feel good and more confident, helps your customer feel more at ease to speak to you, and allows you stand out in a crowd. When you take the time to look good, you convey the message of success, that you take your job seriously, and if you take care of yourself, then you will definitely take care of the customer.

On top of this, looking your best in this industry primarily means two things. The first is professional office attire and second is grooming. For professional attire, make sure your clothes are clean, pressed and fit properly. For gentlemen, a nice fitting pair of pants and long-sleeved shirt looks very pleasant; you could even top it off with a blazer if you feel inclined. For women, a midi dress or skirt, some low heels, and a blazer looks effortlessly professional.

Grooming is usually overlooked but plays a significant role in creating a certain perception of yourself. The best grooming tips for men is, try to keep the hair short and not trendy. You should smell clean and fresh, not too much cologne, clean nails that are preferably kept short. For women, keep hair professional not trendy. The nails should be really simple, smell clean and fresh not too much perfume as some customers are highly sensitive to smells.

In short putting some effort into your appearance does translate to money in the bank as people will respect you and be more inclined to speak to you. In general, the image that you should try to convey with your appearance is world class professionalism, using your attire so that it creates a favorable impression with your client before you talk to them about their insurance needs.

Developing These Habits Will Get Your Closer to Success.

1. Tell the truth to your client, even if it is difficult for you to say. It is better to tell the   avoiding them or beating around the bush and eventually ruining a client/agent relationship.

2. Undersell is the secret that allows customers to purchase coverage they can afford that stays on the books.

3. Take on the whole family as clients, make a note of family members, keep up with them and always look for opportunities to serve.

4. To be able to put the customer's needs first, take care of your own personal finances, save an emergency fund of 6 months to a year's living expenses. Take out some personal life insurance.

"Fight till the last gasp"

-William Shakespeare

Conclusion

Selling is a skill that can be learned. This book attempts to break down the insurance sales process, bit by bit, based on what has worked for me. The first part of the book lists in order, how to acquire a customer and take them through the sales cycle while adding value to the customer and yourself.

The second part of the book is equally important. It has to do with helping you decide what kind of Independent Insurance agent you want to be. Before you pursue the journey to accumulate clients, understand, how your book of business is related to your insurance appointment. You can decide to have a direct appointment, where you own your book of business, take on all the risk to acquire clients, and receive the full compensation directly from the insurance company. Similarly, you could choose to have an Indirect appointment with a group or senior agent, where you may or may not own your book of business, take on a partial risk and share your commissions with the third party.

And finally, the third part of the book deals with personal habits, and how they affect you, your customer and your income. By developing good work habits and processes, you create an environment where success is all but guaranteed.

Thank you for taking the time to read this book. I hope it helps you in your business. This book catalogues the personal experiences of my insurance career, I appreciate you for being a part of this continuing journey.

A final note

It took me a long time to figure all this out, yet the advice is as old as time. Success does not belong to the most intelligent, it belongs to the most consistent. Those that show up, and check off their do list daily will succeed, because that to do list is a step to a goal. What this process told me was goals are attainable to anyone and everyone willing to work for them. Do not give up, because, **you** deserve success. Work for what you want, and you will surely attain it.

Best wishes on your endeavor and may your success be endless!

------Thayü------

Resources

Here are some of the tools that I use for marketing, that might be of use to you.

Leads

www.Salesfully.com

This is a low-cost subscription (29$) based service that provides unlimited business and consumer needs: The leads contain names, addresses, phone numbers, number of employees that you can filter and create a custom list.

https://www.infofree.com/

This is a fee (99$/month) based service that provides unlimited business and consumer leads, business profiles and free CRM

https://www.listshack.com/

This is a fee (50$/month) based service that provides business and consumer leads.

Scripts

https://www.scriptly.me/

Low cost subscription (5$/month). Get help creating sales scripts or borrow from the existing database.

Dialer

https://callhub.io/

A pay as you go predictive automated virtual dialer. I use it to automatically dial multiple numbers at a time. The system only connects to customers who answer the phone.

Made in the USA
Columbia, SC
11 March 2023

13632800R00061